salmonpoetry

*Celebrating 35 Years
of Literary Publishing*

BY THE SAME AUTHOR

POETRY

Kurzpass-Spiel (German-language)

Riverbank City — A Bremen Canvas

NON-FICTION

Song and Democratic Culture

Alive and Kicking: Fußball zwischen England und Deutschland (bi-lingual German/English)

War and Peace: Voices from the Battlefield

TELEVISION FILM

Cool to be Celtic

Granny's Interpreter
IAN WATSON

*for Ray & David,
with love and
very best wishes,
Ian
2/5/2017*

salmonpoetry

Published in 2015 by
Salmon Poetry
Cliffs of Moher, County Clare, Ireland
Website: www.salmonpoetry.com
Email: info@salmonpoetry.com

Copyright © Ian Watson, 2015

ISBN 978-1-910669-03-7

All rights reserved. No part of this publication may be reproduced or transmitted in any form or by any means, electronic or mechanical, including photography, recording, or any information storage or retrieval system, without permission in writing from the publisher. The book is sold subject to the condition that it shall not, by way of trade or otherwise, be lent, resold or otherwise circulated without the publisher's prior consent in any form of binding or cover other than that in which it is published and without a similar condition, including this condition, being imposed on the subsequent purchaser.

COVER PHOTOGRAPHY: Jessie Lendennie
COVER DESIGN & TYPESETTING: *Siobhán Hutson*
Printed in Ireland by Sprint Print

*Salmon Poetry gratefully acknowledges the support of
The Arts Council / An Chomhairle Ealaoín*

for Susanne

Acknowledgements

Thanks are due to the editors of the following magazines and anthologies where some of the texts in this collection have already appeared:

Alive and Kicking, *Bremer Blüten*, *Cyphers*, *Gulliver*, *Hard Times*, *Icarus*, *Irish Pubs*, *Literatur in Bremen*, *Lyrischer Pfad Bremen*, *newleaf*, *Poetry Salzburg Review*, *Prairie Schooner*, *Scarlet Quarterly*, *Skript*, *Stint*, *taz.die tageszeitung*, and *The Troubles in Ireland*.

Some have been read on Radio Bremen's *Augustins Miniaturen*, *Daheim in der Fremde*, *Buten un Binnen*, *Whittaker's Way* and *Heimatfunk*.

Thanks too to my writer friends Michael Augustin, Julia Boll, Simon Makhali, Terry McDonagh, Kirsten Steppat and Elke Marion Weiß for their unflinching support.

Contents

Hedge	11
Bones	12
The Lighthouse	13
On Brandon	15
Pizza on the Somme	16
Spider Breakfast	20
Bat Sonnet	21
Screen	22
Blood on the Tracks	23
Too Late for Letters	24
Pressure Changes	27
Spider Pin Board	28
Volta	29
Bars in Övelgönne	30
Landing	31

A YEAR WITH BREMEN

Saturday Morning, January	33
Glance Beyond February	34
March, from an Intercity	35
Spindrift, April	36
The First of May	37
June in Quelkhorn, Lower Saxony	38
The First of July (Euro '96)	39
Lecture des vacances, August	40
September Attack	41
Wasps, October	42
Buß- und Bettag, November	43
The Sitter, December	44

THE ULSTER WAY

Away Games	47
Supplements	48
Ulster Nights 1969	49
Ulster Haikus	50

Ulster Wedding Vows	51
Belfast Virgins	52
Digging: A Cover Version	53
Squaring Things	54
Home Grown	55
First Performance	57
Saint Patrick's Day	59
Home from Home	60

IN LOW GERMANY

Cameo, Walberberg	65
Kruger's Pub, Dún Chaoin, Kerry	67
The Music Man	68
Pedal Drum	69
Postcards Home	70
Broad Thoughts on Home	71
Granny's Interpreter	72
Holywood Night	74
Against the Grain	75
Hard-boiled	76
Milestones	77
Stones	79
Indian Summer	80
Heimaten	81

THE HILL BEHIND THE HOUSE

And the Bonny Rowan Tree	83
The Hazels	85
Best Man, Cross Country	86
Hares	87
Fugitive	88
Fledged	89
On the Greenisland Shore	90
Departures	91

Hedge

for Pearse Hutchinson

With the engine of the world asleep,
the old men stare out to where the sea is,
sniffing where the wind used to be.

Grief lies like curled leaves on the land,
lies with the lightness of the dead wren in the hedge
on the shoulders of the drinkers.

The hedge is where the schools were,
hunched against the wind
where they could smell the sea.

With the hedge there was no wind; now
without the wind there is no need for hedges.
The dead wren lies with the lightness

of her hatched eggs
in the skeleton of the hedge.
Should the wind return,

she will blow like tumbleweed
down towards Doolin across the field.
The view is a half-moon through branches;

the silence lies like lightness
in the frost, the ash of wren-skull
still as pebbles under ice.

Old sheep sniff unsheared;
the hatched eggs of the dead corn
scratch like voles' feet on cobbles.

Bones

Then on the beach a tiny skull.
I picked the whiteness up
that lodges in my pocket now:

the gentle scratch on finger end
like a hamster sniffing
on my shoulder

caresses but does not console –
I too am picked bare.

The Lighthouse
for Logie Barrow

As far south-west of Belfast as we could be,
breasting the cliff before the morning,
we see the lighthouse –
squat on the rock we know is grey;
wasting its glare on the pulls and drags
of the unresponsive sea;
flaring and dazzling the circling gannets,
the puffins, the cormorants and shags.

I am the truth and the light but not the way.
The darkest place, the Japanese say,
is under the lighthouse.
Our darkest place was living in a history book
where all it took was to mispronounce the alphabet
in the wrong pub at the wrong time,
to have the wrong first name in the wrong street –
and you were history yourself.

Below us on the shingle and the fine white sand we still can't see:
        the skeletons of birds,
        the shells of crabs,
        the clumps of weed,
        bleached wood from South America,
        the shreds of blue nylon rope,
        the plastic Volvic bottles,
        the wading sandpipers,
        the scuttling terns,
        the strutting oystercatchers.

The dark here is still a door into the day to come.
The gaps between the lighthouse lighten
grey by shifting shade of grey.

Crunching and pebble-slipping down to the beach,
we scatter the birds;
we watch the shadows of our boot prints flash
on and off — on and off — on and off
like a northern checkpoint.
Fumbling in the half-light for flat stones
glimpsed in split seconds, we grab one,
hurl and skim and holler.

We turn and tramp towards breakfast,
scraping pictures in the sand,
with the lighthouse flashing our shadows before us
and warming our backs.

And the rest is from history.

On Brandon

for Dorothy Calvert

Ireland is a mountain-top beside the sea. And so
we left the car by a ruined house of nettled stone
and walked five hours and a half, before the cross
came into sight ten yards ahead in the jetting fog
that whipped at us at forty miles an hour.

From the coast's bright sun over dry-stone walls,
we are three thousand feet into that
other world, the hell of damping cold.
Put up your hood, she said, and then:
I think we've reached the sky.
Above the clouds and your feet on Ireland, near on
ten miles and three hours from the silken pint
that warms the mind and dries the boots.

The flesh creeps on the mountain-top.
The cairn, Saint Brendan's pile of stones:
a thousand year's defiance of the
ocean wind and the high-speed fog
that creeps below your anorak and chills your bones.

Pizza on the Somme

to my grandfather, Pte 22497 John Crawford, Highland Light Infantry

WARLOY-BAILLON CEMETERY

Not at the going down
of any sun, but on hot
afternoons, when the sky
breathes only cotton wool
and crickets rub in wheat
and the bonnet scorches;
whenever harvesters in heat
block baking lanes in late July
or when I sit on grass to cool,
I will remember you.

THE SEARCH

After years of wondering and
rolling down through roads in Picardy
flanked by cemeteries,

I'd found you on the internet
in a databank of the dead –
one of three namesakes.

I found the spot on a local map,
called the family together,
then we told our Bremen friends.

Year after year, we'd B&B-ed
eight miles from here and passed
within a mile or two on the *Nationale*.

We came in two carloads
en route to Brittany,
a convoy of German families

stuck flashing behind tractors,
hooting and laughing and sticky:
enlisted as battlefield tourists.

Finding tree-shade to park,
we sobered soon
behind the village church.

The Find

Ingrun softly scans
this orgy of weeding and mowing,
the kempt tending of carnage.

Spruce stones in flowered rows
a touch too narrow for a shoulder
obscure the digging of the hole.

It all got lost behind their holocaust;
but in my home town whole streets
were widowed in a morning in July.

Row I. C. 31

And now we hunker here like
tourists at your grave,
this little German girl and I,
and have our picture taken
for your daughter.

Signing Off

Into the Book of Remembrance
I scratched my name and
Let us sleep now ...

A rush of shame. I'd wanted to leave
some mark, to lift my leg and piss against
that *corner of a foreign field*.

'Casa Nostra', Amiens

Year after year, your great-
grandchildren have spat and pelted
pebbles into this treacle river

at bubbles of maybe trout.
Here is the mosquito hum,
the crouch of anglers,

the wave, the shoulder shrug.
And year after year we have
taken a table at the

pasteria on the river bank.
The women smoke.
We order pizza on the Somme:

Un vin rouge à la maison, une pression.
It's just a river just
another river's name to some.

By Amiens Cathedral

A prisoner of war,
he'd come back here in 'forty-six,
months out of work in Bamberg,

and settled down with a local girl.
His wife tried a few words in German
wrapped in nods and smiles.

When we told of our find,
his interest waned as if that
war before his own was ancient history.

The cathedral has seen a thousand years
and hung out so many flags to dry;
the wire was a blink in the pageant.

CHÂTEAU À QUERRIEU, BED AND BREAKFAST

The chateau stays
untouched by history
but used to making it.

Safe miles behind the
front he never saw,
His Majesty King George

stays unmuddied by the war
he plunged into waging
against a foreign cousin:

pure Shakespeare.
But out in front behind the wire,
the chessmen they call farmers

in Germany chew mud once more
at the breach and *would they were
in an alehouse* in Glasgow.

The day you stumbled
and must have guessed the worst,
the men who sent you out

drank red wine here as we do now.
And this is what I should have
written in the book.

Spider Breakfast

My daughter screams.
I run.
She points:

in the bath a pulsing bullet-hole.
I fetch my piece of card and jam jar
calmly, swiftly like a jaguar,

but pounce uncleanly,
stuffing leg-ends
between enamel and glass

with a postcard of Siena.
Past coin eyes caged
between white fingers,

I walk erect to the patio door
out to where my dark friends wait,
pecking moss, one eye

on early-morning house-lights.
Two legs good:
eight legs bad.

I lob.
I empty the jar in a black rainbow.
My disciples bob and pounce.

They know me;
they call me Tarzan,
Lord of the Blackbirds.

Bat Sonnet

We slept in the old round tower.
Madame reminded us to leave
the rusty turret window open
à cause des chauves-souris.

We'd been in a rush, that night
of the concert in Albi, but they must
have heard us on the gravel
or maybe my turn of the ancient key.

We shrieked as a couple tumbled
past us to their late black buffet.
Later we watched them spin,

then took our turns at hanging
each other upside down –
spiralling blind into the dark.

Screen

On the second visit
the receptionist smiled
but wouldn't meet his gaze.

The specialist, though,
took time to explain
the sharp dialectics of how
positive is negative.

Blood on the Tracks

Children on the line.
Hiss and lightning of train.
In a flash, flat coin.

Remembering,
years later,
Stefan went
to meet the hurricane,
broke like thunder
and burst his father's heart.

Too Late for Letters

in memoriam Dieter Herms 1937-1991

Already you are five months dead
and I never got around to writing down
this eulogy for an old compassionate:
things I never dared to say when you were there
and yet flow out now on to paper to be read
by those who knew and loved you.
It is too late for letters now;
the keyboard is a pale mosaic of tacit thanks and pain.

Bloody great bear of a man,
old friend of better days,
rest somewhere in peace.

It was your anger that attracted me to you first —
a righteous and a life-affirming wrath
(how easily that Bible word slips from the pen);
it was a rage uncannily devoid of hate.
If you had a sin, *Genosse*, it was disdain,
but even this you kept for bureaucrats and Pharisees.
You had the rage of Jesus in the temple;
you could turn over tables with the best.

You were a juggler that I came to love;
there was a balance you could hold between
the three globes you kept spinning in the air:
that anger, the laughter and your settled warmth.

I remember mornings when the wine
had made a garden gnome of you.
Your chest would shrink and when
your chin and beard were pointed up
you seemed somehow smaller than you were,
and vulnerable — even then —
a prematurely wrinkled little boy.
But then some memory of the previous night
would intrude and suddenly ignite
gigantic laughter, and expand you to your proper scale.

What price a simile, a metaphor for your wistful smile?
For it could bring out wrinkles like the crust of mother earth
around a sky-reflecting pool, unleash adagios on the outskirts
    of the ear.
For all your outer rage you were a gentle man.
The sit-in was your forte, *alter Freund*:
firm, flexible but hard to budge;
pushing the politeness of opponents to its limits,
stretching their civilised veneers
to Chinese-lantern paper-thin.

I cannot believe as you believed
that you are here; yet you are here.
Though we have lost you to the stars, the rooms
we teach in sometimes echo with you still.
At meetings where we flail ourselves there booms
a missing baritone: *Freunde, stellt euch nicht so an!*
On Fridays, when the building empties,
I have seen you in the shadows of the neon corridors
and needed your advice, *Kollege*.

If the walls of this academy were strong enough to carry plaques
I would engrave in brass with diamond nibs
the words, 'He was his colleagues' conscience.'
I'd have the students spray on *Sichtbeton* or on the bricks
of pristine admin blocks in paint the colour of blood
graffiti for the bureaucrats: 'He put the wind up you, you pricks.'

And when I ask myself just what it is of you I carry in me now,
I'd say
you helped me shed my fear of conflict like a lizard's skin;
I'd say
your illness taught me to re-shuffle my priorities in life;
I'd say
I have started to stake out the boundaries of my own mortality
with gaudy spangled flags.

But out of all the fragments that I hoard,
out of all the memories I have kept,
out of all the lessons you passed on,
out out beyond our last still Tuesday afternoon,

when I browsed through your bookshelves as you slept,
remains your hardest pain: to lose a child –
the sharpest fear to ever pierce a father's sleep.
And this regret I pass on to my daughter and my son:
that only once in all of both our lives we saw each other weep.

At the end you seemed at times to have no truck with anger;
as you grew weak it fizzled out like ozone into space.
Although: you told me that in spite of all your faith
you found it hard to loosen your grip on life:
Es ist hart, das Loslassen; es ist trotzdem hart.
Yet if you ever railed against your God,
then never once to me.

And then some flash of anger seemed to buoy you up;
foreseeing violence that has since come true,
you warned of those who want to turn the screw
of history back sixty years.
Die Finsternis nimmt zu, die Kräfte nehmen ab.
No, Dieter, there are too many jobs undone;
including some we thought *erledigt* long ago
that now crawl back across our desks to in-trays
filled, God knows, enough with projects in arrears.

I know you heard what friends and colleagues left unsaid
but was transmitted anyway by tears and touch.
We faxed whole paragraphs through fingertips:
the Braille of those who feel more than they can say –
yet how we wish we'd said it anyway.
Too late for letters now.

The keyboard murmurs.
It is nearly done.
I let my song go.
Nothing is exorcised.
The mourning goes on.

As the pain took over, the baritone became a whisper;
your fighting chest became imprisoned in that iron grid.
You did not go gentle, Dieter – but then, you seldom did.

Pressure Changes

Uphill —

it's like playing both halves uphill.
The pull of gravity rises and groans,
lung volume hisses and falls
like a geriatric accordion.

If I were a bike my rims
would be thumping on the cobblestones.
My pump is asthmatic, there's a
leak in the bellows and biceps.

Elsewhere the pressure rises —
under my belt, around the ankles and
where my socks ring shins and calves.
There is a pair of pliers round my heart;
the thump at the temples appals.

In an earlier life I pumped against
the barbell and the medicine ball, where
now I sweat under the weight of my mortality:
pumped out but heavy, lead in my belly.

There is a depression coming from the west —
uphill.

Spider Pin Board

You won't be here when big black spiders
creep from their rusty holes to stretch their legs,
blinking surprise in the stadium lights,
to breathe in cool-warm Old Wives' summer air.

You won't be here when I climb the basement steps
to blink my eyes in the floodlights' green, to
breathe in cooling air from the Champions League:
just me alone against Chelsea and Barcelona.

But you will find a TV bar and friends with hearts
you'll win to green and white to weave new webs
and spin new stories in the salty sandy heath
and sing of Peterswerder where your picture hangs.

There will be big black spiders where you are.
But what are they against a postcard and a jam jar?

Volta

Total eclipse of the moon over Carlisle, Pennsylvania, November 2003

for Joshua Kupetz

In College Street the moon is upside down,
a horizontal sickle, orange brown.

We lurch vibrating down to Harrisburg,
the moon is whole and alabaster white;
but by the time we hit the Route 11
turn-off point, she has a shadow on her lung.

I do a double take, the driver stops.
We stand, illegally, and stare. He asks,
— *And will you see this over there in Europe?*
— *Well, them not me, I'm here this week with you.*

Outside the Market Cross, I take another peek:
a fat blood orange in a silver dish.
I pull my collar up and make a wish:
— *I'll peel and eat you in the coming week.*

Bars in Övelgönne

I live by the tidal Elbe.
I watch the ships pass.
I learn to read the funnels.
I am an expert on ensigns and flags.

I live with a river pilot's son;
Holger teaches me things.
He points; I learn.
We observe. We wave.

On Sundays it is we who are
the watched; the walkers
on their way to coffee stare
in our window as they pass.

They observe; they point —
Da trinkt einer Kaffee.
We stare; sometimes we wave
like gorillas behind bars.

One Sunday, Holger writes
Bitte nicht füttern!
I talk him out of throwing
bananas. We learn; we wave.

Landing

Before the trees appeared
under the porthole like fresh-rinsed
parsley, there were wet Dutch roads
like audio cassette tape spilled out
along the plain between the
towns of Lego brick.

And by the time the trees were broccoli
and the roads were German broadband tape
below our wheels, I stared at my fingers linked
to mime indifference on my lap.

But at the smoky screech,
my guts, as they always do, had set
their mind on spilling out
along the plane.

A YEAR WITH BREMEN

Saturday Morning, January

Big fat heavy flakes
fall into a sea of cold white:
my daughter's breakfast.

Big fat heavy flakes
packed into a sea of cold white:
my daughter's snowbear.

Glance Beyond February
(a five by five by five)

An upright strip of what in ten days' time
might well be sunshine creeps from left to right
across my bookshelves. Just a Penguin wide
a quarter of an hour ago, it swells
to four and three eighths inches, browsing and

caressing lightly two Leitz files, *The Faber
Book of Ballads, Penguin Book of English
Verse*, a German-English dictionary,
my Bible, Seamus Heaney's *North* and Thompson's
Making of the English Working Class.

It shrinks again and inches unwarm down
the window frame towards the street, where in
another quarter of an hour the sun
will breathe cold light onto the house-front brick
just behind my back. But unwarmed black

and goose-bump chestnuts fail to take the hint;
they have forgotten sweating afternoons
of last July, when they would wear their leaves
like stifling scarves and wish that they could moult
like sheepdogs or be shorn like sheep. Inside,

I jog my random access memory of
that human sense of clock and calendar
that lets me glance beyond the present tense.
I listen to the herald's voice. The spring's
kick-start arrives as writing on my wall.

March, from an Intercity

The land is under water
between Osnabrück and Münster.
It is a sluggish landscape this time of year;
to left and right the wet fields lie
like mildewed mirrors of the pewter sky,
turning it slate by sleight of hand.
Oh, but it's the wetness ...

Behind my shoulder, Bremen slips away
downward on a dull rolling stair:
lead, lead the skyless cloud, the land all silver grey.
Once-silver silos slide in/out, in and out,
entering and leaving our lives.
Oh, but it's the wetness and the flatness ...

Flat rain starts to spit, then hack and
slash the double window; geese in mossy
concrete yards flash like paper hankies
wind-caught in chicken wire.
Oh, but it's the wetness and the flatness
and the skating endlessness.

Skiting through the damp backyards of places
motorways don't reach, we shutter-click
on split-second movements we store away as
opening shots of a dozen movie scripts:
a man weeping opens a car door;
two old men with shotguns
climb a barbed-wire fence.

The rivers swell an inch an hour to kiss
the dykes. A hundred miles south-west of here,
the Rhine caresses his cathedral.
There'll be soldiers with sandbags on the dykes.
There'll be a rolling up of basement carpets
and a rolling out of Red Cross blankets.
There'll be wet feet in the Neustadt tonight.

Spindrift, April

Well slept, we clear the breakfast things away.
Dreamily and gently rinsing,
I glance down from the kitchen window
on to the spindly lawn,
where the neighbours' tomcat wrestles
with enemies of his imagination.

Pow!   Biff!   Bam!
Bandit dogs are made to bite the dust and
Wham!
the Apache bulldog behind him gets
an elbow in the face and
Slam!
the butterfly in the Richard Widmark part
goes to meet its fate –
once upon a time in the west.

And in the moment of glory
(as the cat wipes his mouth on his dusty sleeve
and hears on the horizon
bugles of the Seventh Feline Cavalry
arriving – as ever – a tad too late)

to the left, unseen, unsung by heroes
at Match-of-the-Day action-replay speed
in a hushed and unstoppable spiral,
white and silently, modestly
yielding right of way for the curling embryo leaves of May,
the first blossom falls from the pear tree.

The six seconds it will take
to its first and last touchdown
are its crossing of the bar.

The First of May

With the sleeve-stroking tenderness of former lovers,
we meet again this year on the First of May,
down streets where once we unfurled banners,
chanting our message in unison
in that very far from tender way.

Today we push Dutch bicycles,
careful only of the heels of those in front.
Beside us, my son rides his own bike;
your daughter inspects her union balloon.

Other people's grown-up children
chant on cobbled tramlines now;
for them the act itself is all there is.
Their slogans are familiarly new,
though black now dominates where
then the air was furled in red.
The rhythm stays: hushed, persistent,
but gentler, warmer than ours was.

Not taking care, my son
rides into the calves of a girl in black.
She starts and smiles and strokes his hair.
He takes the leaflet she offers;
it will make another paper plane –
but I will read it first.

June in Quelkhorn, Lower Saxony
for Thomas and Priscilla Metscher

Your land is dry. The sweet-corn leaves
all gossip in the flabby wind. The hair
and shoulders of a cyclist slit the fields
of ripish maize three hundred yards afar.

The heat-haze merges with the ocean of
the waving barleycorn. Horizons blur,
spumed lines of poplar trees between the soft
and sunflower sea and hanging shot-silk air.

Morosely periscoping ochre pools,
a trawling tractor's perspex conning tower
disturbs the quivering, circling hawk's patrols.

A phrase like *bathed in light* might seem forspent
to those who pose the view that metaphor
must always ring as new with rhymes unkent.

The First of July (Euro '96)

Exactly eighty years, to the afternoon,
after his Scottish great-grandfather
fell to the ratatat ratatat ratatat tat
of his mother's grandfather's platoon,

my German son stands on the mobile steps
below a Euro-built Lufthansa airbus,
welcoming home our local club's
four European Nations champions:

Eilts, Bode, Reck and Todt.

And in his hand a tricolour flag
that none of his German great-
grandfather's comrades would have
recognised as their own.

Lecture des Vacances, August

Reading Longley's 'Northern Lights' in Guimorais,
I smell the Ulster fry and smoky turf,
but out behind the mobile homes I hear the gulls,
and squeals of Breton girls in surf.

September Attack

They stand there spindle-legged,
as delicate as young giraffes;
but in flight they are substantial —
lead zeppelins.

They will not dive like gannets on their prey
or plummet from a tree to kill their dinner first;
but sidle sharkly up to fallen pears already burst,
their sideways flight recalling helicopters:
gunship slalom cruising
                              — apocalypse now.

Wasps, October

Wasps
are perishing in dustbins
expiring on window-sills
passing away in wet ash-filled cardboard cups.

Wasps
caught short by cold-snap nights
drown slowly and lazily in balding hedges
with nowhere to hide
and nothing to die respectably under.

Wasps
stinging their way to heaven
must suffer their hell before they go:

writhing buzzing spinning through October
on the pavements next to street-lamps
in the bedrooms inside slippers
in the gutters beside bread-crusts
in the kitchens behind floor-cloths
in the gardens among trowels
in the bathrooms between towels
in the drawers under sweaters

the death-whine of summer.

Buß- und Bettag, November

There is in Bremen a bronchitic time
that is neither hell nor winter,
but an all-consuming purgatory
of grey –
repent and pray.

Huddled boys at bus-stops in the fog
cough fog in clouds. In clouds
the sky has fallen under a weight of sins
we have to purge. We urge
the penance that we have to pay –
repent and pray.

All afternoon the sodium lamp
can scarcely penetrate a damp
that crawls on hands and knees
and creeps in under cafe doors
to cool your tea; my song
can hardly penetrate the grey.
Was ever such a day
so short? Was ever such a day
so long?
Repent and pray.

The graveyard is ankle-deep in what
is left of summer shade
now made black compost by the wet
that sticks with clay
to once-black boots.
And all around the roots
sackcloth and sodden ash –
repent and pray.
The bells of Hastedt groan and clash –
Atone! Atone!

The Day of Repentance and Prayer, until recently a public holiday
in Germany, usually on the third Wednesday in November

The Sitter, December

Karate-chopped by frost,
rhododendron leaves hang limp
like bats in chloroform.

The earth is tungsten hard.
The garden hibernates —
except for one red-breasted neighbour
posing for a Christmas card.

THE ULSTER WAY

Away Games

I hear the accents of home in a Leicester pub,
ordering a pint. – *Right you are, Mick,*
says the landlord. – *What'd you say? Mick? Me?
No way! I'm an Ulsterman, squire, loyal and true.*
– *Sorry, mate, no offence.* A shrug,
uninterested at best, at worst a hint of sneer.

It's a long long way from Ballyclare to here.
And far from the kerbstones in red, white and blue
and far from the sashes and the silver band,
we're all Micks in the motherland.

In a folk club above a bar in Travemünde,
I hear the old familiar voice again,
banging out *The Jolly Beggarman* and *Arthur McBride*
in sandpaper quarter-tones.
And when we say hello, his name betrays him first:
Scots Lowland, the sandy-haired heartland.
His family have a chemist's in Coleraine.

Supping the black nectar of exile
and teaching the local children English,
far from the orange and purple bunting
and far from the Lambeg drums and *Dolly's Bray*,
we all want to be Paddies when we're playing away.

Supplements

(Northeast Ireland Region only)

Thou shalt keep a low profile.

Thou shalt not cause a fuss.

Thou shalt not cause other people unnecessary bother even though they would actually enjoy helping.

Thou shalt find out first what the others want before thou sayest thyself.

If thou art asked if thou wantest another cup of tea, thou shalt not say Yes if the pot has to be refilled.

Thou shalt not change water into wine.

Thou shalt not complain to the waitress even when thou knowest thou ordered something else.

Thou shalt not always say what thou thinkest.

Thou shalt only occasionally say what thou feelest.

Thou shalt only feel when necessary.

Ulster Nights 1969

1 July

Oh Jesus, not the drums again;
I couldn't bear the drums.
Another night of orange summer thunder
drifting over fields and under
clouds of slanting Antrim rain,
lifting the latches of barns,
rumbling in slumbering children's dreams,
rattling the doorknobs,
throbbing down the hedges,
pulsing over water,
soothing sleeping cattle,
echoed off the high-rise,
beating out the tribal tattoo of fear.

1 December

Midnight bumps in the winter night
that light the sleeping windows on Carnmoney Hill,
and steam that writhes and rises and hangs
above wet soldiers' woollen hands,
blown and clapped in the backs of vans,
have taught our children that history hurts.

Ulster Haikus

UNDER SIEGE
(1994)

Antediluvian;
flat caps, flat vowels, flat earth:
Loyalist Ulster.

YES VOTE
(22 May 1998)

I'd rather have a
cross-border body than a
cross border collie.

LIFESTYLE
(November 1999)

But if anything
sums up the Ulster life-code,
it is deference.

Ulster Wedding Vows

I do, so I do.
So do I, so I do.

Belfast Virgins

Some cross their arms across their breasts
and stoop down to the shops for cigarettes,
some arm-in-arm three-legged in the street.

Some even take their curlers out
and seem as though they've kept them in;
some never learn to swim.

Some parallel their legs at dances
and practise surreptitious glances,
some stay for ever buttoned up in cars.

Some take their teddy bears on honeymoon
and lay them on their marriage beds,
some take their mothers with them in their heads.

Digging: A Cover Version
for S.H.

Pushing off from the
first poem in your first book,
I have grown to enjoy
the myriad of ways and means
to call a spade a spade.

Squaring Things
for S.H., i.M.

What you saw then out on the road beyond
Coleraine was mine as well, although derived
and fed on homesickness and Barber's *Adagio*

that oozed from the hire-car radio, and by the sun
above black snow clouds up behind Sliabh Liag,
where the mountain meets the sea. Namely:

that what is glimpsed – the micro-second whoosh,
that thrust – is what we have already known.
The sighting sleeps inside us in a pod;

the poem's just the thumbs that open it.
Now, stoked up on *Seeing Things,* I write
this down. The book was just the prod.

Home Grown

for Cecile Sandten

December in Portrush:
back in the old home
it's blasts of salty rain and short
afternoons at the scorching fire
of the Harbour Bar,

where Simmons and Heaney once pulled
on pipes and pints and threads
of politics and conversation.
It was a time for curtains pulled
and birthdays where the cloakroom steamed
with sodden coats and scarves.

When I recall that time, I see you
with your back to Europe,
tiny below the Causeway cliffs,
catching on the Atlantic wind
Satanic Verses, maybe
snatches of Grace Nichols rhymes,
the odd snippet of Derek Walcott,
voices from Sujata Bhatt, pain-cries
from Caryl Philips' *Crossing the River*.

We sent you there and since then
the world has been your library.
Pushed from the Bremen nest,
you flew. You grew to kiss
the muse of every continent.
We pushed and saw you soar.

Visiting, I swear
I saw your gift unfold,
as if the Causeway Coast
kick-started you, out there

on the edge of the edge
of the edge of Europe.

You came home grown.
You too have crossed the river now
from where the students live.
You have returned unfurled
and here, on short
December afternoons,
our library is now your world.

Refuel and fly.

First Performance

on hearing Matthias Wichmann's 'Movements'

It was as if I'd heard your piece
before. Don't get me wrong: not that
it reminded me of other tunes. Rather,
it was as if it had always flowed in me
here and in hard winters somewhere else.

The moment the accordion breathes
and the heart lifts above the dark
out beyond the freezing fog
and crackling leaves outside
in the museum garden,

the poems rise unbidden
like desire. And now I will not
sleep. This hour I give you
and these lines. You have
charted me home:

Back to Portrush again –
where the drizzle crystallises
into ice blown off the sea;
where grubby seagulls huddle
grumpily on white cliff shelves.

I dream we'll all meet there one night,
with Philip Glass and Liam Óg O'Flynn,
Danny Federici and Arvo Pärt. We'll link up
arm and sleeve and arm, a supergroup
in woollen coats and long hot scarves.

We'll hear the ghosts of Rory Gallagher
and Lynott on the wind. In a long line,
we'll brazen out Atlantic fog
to where the fire is by the ocean
and the window blazes like the northern star,

and lilt a step, roar out a song
and stumble over ropes strung out
along the whole width of the quay —
out towards the Harbour Bar.

Then we'll show that Mikis
Theodorakis how to sink a pint.

Saint Patrick's Day

Just before the equinox,
the weather comes
in waves of wickedness.

Passing Sliabh Mis in the
minibus on the day of days,
I feel no metaphors.
The mountain where he kept the sheep
is only still a mountain.

I have not come out
of hibernation yet.

Home from Home

for Sean Mullan

1. AT THE PINK HOUSE

Bamboozled by a maze of high-hedge roads
that drove us up past Fanad lighthouse twice,
we arrived in from Sligo at six o'clock
to the welcome, the craic and the dark dark pints.

2. COLLIES

White-eyebrowed, foul-mouthed collies
bark the wheels off the passing cars
and pass the ever-identical day away.
With legs as short as their tempers,
they take their servility out on the sheep.

They'll greet you with a milquetoast wagging tail
and with their heads ducked sideways to the right.
They half expect a blow and so are humbly glad,
grateful for the ruffle of their coat;
but it's on the thin, capped man they keep
one eye. They wait for his nod of approval.

3. NIGHT

Night's kiss lingers now on Fanad.
A thud of engine, whimper of the timber,
the green light slides, the boat, unseen,
patrols the night for daily bread of fish.
The deceptive calm of the north-west night
can plunder men and eat armadas whole –
the nescient power of a million tons of sea.

Into the silence of the evening hill,
for a moment an opened door spills
merriment: on the breeze a snatch of bark
and on the dark a hint of chill.
Oh Sean, I'd easy bid this townland home,
and peel Lough Swilly's thin banana moon
where it hangs over black Inishowen tonight –
over thistle and whin and the ink-thick sea.

4. Borders

Next day you left for Derry
and crossed without effort from home to home
over the barbed-wire zig-zag scar
that is more than just a county line
to your home in a country that is just
half yours – was mine and is no longer;
for robbed of my past by the history books
of Cromwell, Nelson and the Butcher Duke,
and robbed of my language, I left.

5. An Honest Ulsterman

If Ireland is a proud old woman
– for no island is a man –
I am the fourth green field.
But am I blighted by a stranger's hand
or am I the stranger?

I am a land within a land;
I am the top red-hand corner,
the place that has to stay unnamed
because naming it reveals your tribe.
I am the fourth green field.

6. OFF SHORE

Others that never were have liked
to call themselves an island race;
and yet their hearts of oak were often Irish,

shorn from forests that were ours
to lie salt-saturated on the continental shelves,
sodden like the peat bogs we were left with.

And after Drake had singed King Philip's beard,
our coasts destroyed the Spanish fleet themselves.
If England won the island race, the also-rans are running still.

7. ALONE

Wednesday:
without you, up to the ankles in Fanad bog,
we crossed the round mountain to the lighthouse,
loving to be here but longing for Bremen,
as if July was just a cease-fire,
only a close-season, honeymoon limbo time
before the wetness of cobbles and
the flatness of hanseatic working days.

8. WILD GEESE

But it's not just through Lough Foyle:
Edward Carson's zig-zag cuts across us all –
barbed wire in all our heads;
the pencilled border neither of us wants.

And it borders on the criminal that it took a cobbled
tourist town, this Legoland of pretty façades
in which we lived two miles apart for all that time
to hitch us over the border between our growings-up.

For we left, Sean, you and I.
Half-baked and curious we came to the land
of the peat-bog and the sluggish canal,
to this flat old hawker of a city that squats

behind her market stalls and buys and sells,
that sits on a bag of treasures raised
from plunder, tricks and taxes –
and feeds and clothes me.

Coming from where we do,
one sentence resonates as new:
Wir gehen nach Bremen;
etwas Besseres als den Tod findest Du überall. *

So cross again, Sean, from home to home to home:
rough likeable Fanad
tough unspikeable Derry
flat bikeable Bremen.

---

* From the Grimms' fairytale The Bremen Town Musicians: 'You had better go with us to Bremen. You're sure to find something better than death somewhere else.'

IN LOW GERMANY

Cameo, Walberberg

for Marijke Brouwer

Sunday evening
Walberberg tram stop
halfway between
Cologne and Bonn
half six or thereabouts.
The conference is over –
I'm homeward bound.

Silver-grey schoolmaster's
well-groomed wavy hair
genuine Mackintosh coat and
real MacDonald tartan scarf.
I remember him from
the Q and A with Julian Barnes.

>   *—You were at the seminar, were you not?*
>   *—Yup.*
>   *—You're ... Irish, aren't you?*
>   *— Mmh.*
>   *—We go over there every year*
>   *A boat on the Shannon, you know*
>   *Fishing*
>   *Peace and quiet*
>   *Wunderbar*
>   *Like the people there*
>   *Warm, chatty, friendly ...*
>   *Not like here*
>   *And always this ... calm*
>   *What we lack here*
>   *No ... stress*
>   *Not like here*
>   *Take their time*
>   *Do everything ... mañana*
>   *Not like here.*

Rocks back on his heels
glares at his watch
and then at the empty horizon.

Eighteen thirty-four. Damn.
It should have been here at twenty-nine.
In Cologne on a Sunday
there's just no relying on the tram.

Kruger's Pub, Dún Chaoin, Kerry

Wet-night back-room tourists:
Maoists, purists from Heidelberg,
expecting to hear the 'Internationale'
on the genuine sheepskin pipes;

their faces contorted with disdain
as the wee man played *'Just for you'*,
on a red Italian accordion,
'The Green Hills of Antrim'.

Too much fithery idle doo
and not enough Aeolian mode;
think what this part of the country could be
with a little bit less of that filthy black beer
and a little more *classenbevusstzine*!

The Music Man

for Georg Schroll

Dog barks dance and skim
like flat stones flung in relay
out across the turf from farm to farm.
The music rises from the dykes and fields.
In stifling rooms, tunes of O'Carolan's
resonate across the years.
There is a peat fire here, the beer is warm;
a bodhrán booms. It could be inland Clare,
but the gig is on the flat North German plain.

In the flatlands, like missionaries we came,
driving as hard as the fog allowed
to a school far out in Eastern Frisia
where Andy Irvine played.

Bands come and go,
the music stays, the music changes;
the music grows and
friendship is the prize
for treating the music with respect.

The locals listen to the Kerry Slides.
The music rises from the dykes and fields
and those who've listened put their hands together.
You brought my songs and jigs and reels
to the pubs and school-halls of the flatlands.

Pedal Drum

Thanks for the bodhrán.
I strapped it on to the bike
and played with my feet –

for all the way home
we rattled out a slip jig
on the cold cobbles.

Postcards Home

Eichstätt

By night, in this small Bavarian town,
I have not felt so safe since I left Bremen.
By day, I have not felt so insecure
since I left Belfast.

Aberystwyth Promenade

The gales in Wales
flail malely
on the rails.

Albert to Bapaume, Picardy

Eccentric hedges
in ripe wheat reveal themselves
as former trenches.

Portmuck, County Antrim

They spin the sea's breath,
weaving it into music
at the Poets' House.

At the Luther House

Here in Halle/Wittenberg
where the cropped skulls shout and sing,
they could do with a short sharp shock
of Martin Luther King.

Homesick

I never looked on life abroad
as exile or as hell,
till the night that Danny Blanchflower died
and there was nobody here to tell.

Broad Thoughts on Home

Clichés like
Home is where the heart is
do sometimes take flight and,
when you're least expecting them,
catch your pencil unawares.

And so, if
I were just to sit and
scan out what I really
feel, I fear I might just write,
Wish you were here.

Granny's Interpreter

No sooner do I have my contact lenses in,
every morning at the mirror, than
I pull my second self over me like a shirt.
My daughter calls me, unsuspecting.
How could her *Papi* be an alien?

At lunchtime on the *Bahnhofsplatz*
I catch a phrase of my mother's tongue
and pull my first self like a flick-knife from my heart.
I offer my services as travel guide
to jovial compatriots who've gone astray.
You certainly know your way around.
How long have you been in these parts?

In the evening I intervene, the one ear
stuck hot to the child's and the phone.
I transmit the second-hand communiqués
of Batman masks, Ghostbusters, leaps from diving boards,
or Judo training, new piano skills and school.
For I am Granny's interpreter;
I translate my son for my mother.

Mother tongue and mother's milk,
my song coagulates to buttermilk.

Again the talk comes round to the Troubles
round the big round table in Gerken's bar tonight.
My Bremen mates berate the Irish and the Slavs:
But how can people in Europe today
smash each other's skulls in for a country's name?
groans a well-meaning regular.
I freeze and sigh into my *Holsten Light*.

Back home in the Jordanstown Inn I retell
how the kids hacked holes in the Berlin Wall.
So how do youse in Germany see the way

that Europe's shaping up? a guy I went to school with asks.
I look away to catch the barman's eye
And order another round of stout
that now tastes just a wee bit of betrayal.
In every foreign correspondent
schemes an embryo double agent.

Since the day at Cultra when, reaching for a
picnic coffee flask on a tourist trip back one July,
I inadvertently told my mother we'd
be leaving for 'home' in a couple of days,
she too has begun to talk in German in my dreams.

Holywood Night

Across the hidden lough, the sodium lights
are jangling orange in the dark brown air.
A quiet calm is on the water.

Up on the mountain he cannot see,
cars snuffle like ladybirds with
miners' helmet lamps in County Down.

There is a dampness lingering over the land.
From the black breathing sea I feel
the sighs and groans of small boats.
The ferries chug their lorry loads from Scotland.

And I know all this in Germany –
listening with my father's eyes
as he scans the bay window of home
with the phone in his hand.

Against the Grain

The child's face was never softer than when after I had shaved.'
(Bernard Mac Laverty, 'Father and Son')

For special times
I give myself
the double shave
against the grain

and for an hour or two
I am as smooth
as any metaphor of babies' bums
until the stubble comes.

Each day I scrape
your memory off
into the porcelain

but leave behind black
pepper dots like heartbreak's rubble
that grow against the grain
of memory and will.

Hard-boiled

The last mosquitoes of the year
sew the air with a giant thread,
dipping and soaring.

Five crows in goose formation
go to do mischief over the river,
like work someone over.

The wren in the ivy, knowing
the cat will not strike while I am here,
begins a slanging match.

Taking the egg from my anorak,
I shift it from hand to hand to cool,
then start to peel and salt.

Milestones

for Peter

Freezing rain south-west of Bremen
fading into the fog
of the Teutoburger Wald
melting into motorway salt

Dortmund eighty-five kilometres
pines to the right of us
pines to the left
and not a sparrow hawk moving

Change of shift at Münsterland
a yawn   a pee   a stretch
he re-adjusts the driver's seat
to fit those longer legs

Dortmund forty-two
Münster   Dülmen   Recklinghausen
Herne   Bochum   Wattenscheid

Now I doze in the
Ruhrpott rush-hour
Mines to the right of us
mines to the left
and never a pit-head turning

A hundred and thirty
A hundred and twenty
Ninety
Eighty
Sixty
road works at the turn-off
to Schalke

Bochum to the right of us
Bochum to the left
and not a drop to drink

Essen-Kray
Essen-Frillendorf
Filtering into the A52
Essen-Bergershausen
Junction 29 – Essen-Süd
Essen-Rüttenscheid
Essen-Haarzopf
Margaretenhöhe

Shifting down through
icicled lights
right-hand slipslide
urban slush
slowdown
handbrake
exhale
made it
gimme five

For the first time
I share the driving
with my son

Stones

I wish you stones,
brown comfort for the hand —
not cold or hard
but cream and heavy
warm and round:
striped pebbles on a strand.

I wish you sun and solid ground.

Indian Summer

for Hannah

Born between the summer and the busy spider time,
when holidays are born again on afternoons
but fade to fall before we've had our tea,
you bring each year your sun-bathed birthday:
cake and coffee on a cool damp lawn; wasps sipping
sleepily on juicy grass or just inspecting plums.

All this is yours,
all this we share with you:
this tiny garden and this sun.

So when November fogs begin to clog up airports; and
when Boxing Day dissolves into the drizzle of a boring
    afternoon;
when January blows the greedy gulls and Irish ferries off
    their course;
when February snows glaze over cobbles till you have to
squeal and hang on to your friends;
think of those self-same round plastic tables,
sun-bathed and servietted, served with cheese-cake,
warm and cool, between the flowering cherry and the deck.

All this is yours,
all this we share with you:
this tiny garden and this sun.

And when the Mad March Hare
has chased the last leaves from the trees and left them bare
at the dead-end of the year, when skies are grey,
remember coffee and cake and folding chairs
on a cool damp lawn, when the world was one.

Forget the busy spiders;
forget the cruising wasps:
just live the tiny garden and the sun.

Heimaten

'What's the plural of *home*, Holmes?'

'Homes.'

'*Homes*, Holmes?'

'Elementary, my dear Watson.'

THE HILL BEHIND THE HOUSE

And the Bonny Rowan Tree

You stoop almost to the ground to get through the hole in the hedge from the garden to the field, minding the new barbed wire but scratching your face as you go. Straightening, you stretch and look towards the hill. The ground behind the garden has been churned up by the bullocks who have been at the laurel leaves, and the herd part to let you through, but two are curious enough to rub up against you. This terrified you as a child, but now you are immune to their stupidity; it is not the persistent curiosity of the cat. One *Shoo!* scatters them, making a dog bark somewhere. At a back window of one of the terrace houses, a curtain moves. First the going is flat, through wettish ground and cow pats, then the climb begins. You see above you the hazel wood hanging on the mountain. As you rise, the sea – the flat channel that takes ships up to the city – comes into view with the hills of the county on the other side. White horses on the water show the wind from the north west. Two small yachts court a ferry from Scotland.

You pass the first rocks and the sheep. The hazels get nearer and, between them, the single mountain ashes, berried in flame. The going gets steeper and soon you have to use your hands. Once, your grasp slips on a hazel branch and you skite and skelter down a few feet on your right, leaving the back of the trouser leg brown from calf to thigh. Every other moment a rabbit scatters, the first few times raising the hairs on the back of your neck. But this time it is not night. Today, between the branches you can still see the ferry. Everything will be alright. With the cliff face of the mountain above you in the sun you get and keep your orientation.

Everything is as it was. When you find the trickle of the source you used to think was a waterfall, you know that the rowan tree you are looking for will not be far. You creep across the mountain in the cover of the hazels, constantly slipping down to the right, once almost turning your ankle. By the time you see it you are so close that it is your next grip-hold. You hug the trunk and rest for a few seconds, before looking for the initials. They are a faint ghost, overgrown but visible – only just. You clear the ground of stones and wood and sit. You lean your back against the bark and know that this is where it will begin.

The Hazels

Neither nuts nor blossoms,
not green serrated leaves –
it is the winter I remember:

smooth winter buds
and grey and yellow catkins
hanging in the mountain's wind.

We slithered aiming
home-cut hazel rifles,
wiping noses on a sleeve.

Wild in the wild woods,
we fought and fired,
as boys will do or did.

There is no cover in the winter;
on the cold mountain
we were exposed to shots

but also to the gaze
of mothers in control
at kitchen windows.

Best Man, Cross Country

Ingleby Kernaghan, 1948-2008

The boy came out of the fog.
I heard the pounding breathing, next
the slap of rubber wet on tarmac –
then the grunt.

It was the black square glasses I saw first,
then the long dark flapping hair:
yer man running with the slightest limp.
He was the business – best man, cross country.

I remember gleaming calves and thighs
like pistons steaming in the gloom, the crouching
shoulders carrying a weight you couldn't see.
The brow was always furrowed.

He was a thudding ghost, the running
phantom of the Knockagh, the master
of the hills, the god of gain through pain.
I remember the back of a green vest.

Go round one more time, I shouted.
Then he was gone.

Hares

Only a month ago I watched them play
together in the droppings of the trees,
testing their legs, preparing each other
for spring and procreation.

But on the Knockagh road the hares are dying now;
so many – nearly every night there's one –
stretched on the road like legs of bacon
dropped by a swerving lorry.

Tonight, two more beside the hedge,
stopped short together in their stride;
outstretched, as if in death they would decide
to chase on down the way they had intended.

A leap in the dark had ended.
In death they ran in keeping with their lives;
swerving in panic into the lights,
full braking before the other edge
together.

Fugitive

The bog has been known to swallow walkers to above the waist;
I have seen friends yelping downwards into glar.
The stories say it has devoured as many running
highwaymen as running highwaymen escaped.
It has digested stumbling men and held them for a year,
and let them surface later, bloated,
scared eyes bulging out and staring,
to be dried out, nailed in and buried again.

Yet it has given refuge too,
shielded so much panting running,
erased so many sole-prints,
helped so many foxes to defect.

The night mist sheltered Brian Sweeney
until his cough betrayed him to their dogs
and they dragged him cringing from his cave
and tied his blue hands behind him
and took him down to Carrick to be hanged.
But when they hanged Brian Sweeney,
they could not cure his cough;
for I have heard him in the fog
that has enwrapped me too
and watched my every move.

I have no dogs to betray him
and my tongue has been tied.

Brian Sweeney was a highwayman who hid out in a cave on Knockagh mountain above our village. His ghost reputedly coughs on dark foggy nights on the hill, for legend has it that his cough betrayed him in the fog. Once in my teens I was alone enough on Knockagh at night to hear him behind me.

Fledged

Still and twisted, a damaged wren
stunned by a last-ditch flight into
a window pane, thin-skinned and bruised,
my mother lies with just a flutter
of a smile. And the busybody gardener
and turner over of leaves is now as light
as a twig, her shell mottled and pale.

*Why does God give you bairns and then
they go away?* she asks, pecking a tiny beak
into my prodigal emigrant guilt.

In here, she carries her name on her wrist.
I hold her crooked hand, my touch as light
as her arthritic bones: now both of us
finally leaving the nest.

On the Greenisland Shore

Suddenly, before us,
a solid rainbow
earthed in the Knockagh and the lough
in all the colours of the basket
we'd decided on for the coffin –
from roses to pinks to lilies to lilac –
and behind us a January sun
of yellow freesias.

Hooked on your arm, your basket
was a solid rainbow:
geranium and holly berry, sunflower, primrose,
primula, lavender, pansy and hyacinth –
and in the autumn asters, bark,
dried sycamore and chestnut brown
earthed in the present and the past.

The rainbow took us back:
all the colours of the world
except that black that carries rain.

And at the last
the freesias
to ease the pain.

Departures

I slide down the gears of the Corsa as the exit approaches. Black below me, the Lagan oozes from right to left as I leave Antrim for Down. There's that drizzle again, the one I know only from Northern Germany and Northern Ireland: not quite rain at all but somehow more than fog. The air and the road surface get only so damp that I have to keep flipping the wipers on at irregular intervals. If I put them on repeat, they squeak, and if I turn them off, the screen is suddenly fuzzy and full of brake lights. To my left I briefly catch the lights of the ferry, the only escape in the old days, now a high-speed hydrofoil. I'm touching down into East Belfast, bumper to bumper at what up here they still call forty-five miles an hour, on what, when I lived here, would have seemed like an Los Angeles freeway. Soon, to my right, the Oval, where in September 1967 I saw Glentoran hold Benfica to a 1–1 draw – the good old days before those bad old days.

One more kilometre on home soil. Already my mind is on the flight; the first short hop is from George Best to Liverpool John Lennon, airports named after two of Dad's *personae* most *non gratae*. The second is to another timezone, another world. I am crossing again from home to home. Already my heart is looking out for the woman in the crowd who will come and take my bag. Goodbye to Dad and goodbye to the right-hand drive, goodbye to Vauxhall and welcome to Opel land. All the cars on the rental lot are shiny black on this shiny black night. In the glare the boy overlooks the scores on the wing; I hand over the key and we smile.

During this fortnight I've lived off things the Germans don't do as well: bacon, intelligent sitcoms, eye contact with strangers, holding doors open – and biscuits. My bag clonks with plain chocolate digestives, Marmite and Ulster smiles. I push it over to the girl at the desk. It reads fourteen point seven. She smiles and I jog relieved to the gate, as if in training for tomorrow's home match – Borussia Mönchengladbach. There is a book in all this; I lean back on the next available pillar and know that this is where it will all begin again.

Photograph by Trish P. Schultz.

IAN WATSON was born in Greenisland, Co. Antrim and now lives in Bremen, North-West Germany. Since the seventies, he has been writing and publishing poems, articles and reviews in anthologies and magazines in Ireland, Britain, Germany, Austria and the United States. *Kurzpass-Spiel*, a German-language collection of poems and micro-prose on football, was published in 2011 by Kellner, and *Riverbank City – A Bremen Canvas*, a volume of English-language poems about his second home, came out with Blaupause Books in 2013. Some of his poems have been translated into German by Jürgen Dierking for both print and radio performance. He has, in turn, translated Heinrich Böll, Arne Rautenberg and Hans Meier into English and poems by Harry Clifton into German.

His non-fiction includes *Song and Democratic Culture* (Croom Helm/St. Martin's Press, New York 1983), the bilingual *Alive and Kicking: Fußball zwischen England und Deutschland* (Argument Verlag, Berlin 1994; co-edited with Diethelm Knauf and Jürgen Dragowski) and two teaching texts: *War and Peace: Voices from the Battlefield* (Klett, Stuttgart 1995); and *Riverbank City: Teaching Material – Ideas, exercises and projects for poetry and local history in English language learning* (Blaupause Books, Hamburg 2014).

He has worked freelance for radio and in 1999, with Marcus Behrens, he made the documentary *Cool to be Celtic* (62 Min.) on Irish popular music for the Franco-German television channel arte. In 1994 he founded newleaf Press and *newleaf* magazine, which he edited with Simon Makhali and Julia Boll. He is vice-chairman of the Virtual Literature House in Bremen.